ART WITH FOUND MATERIALS

John Lancaster

Consultant: Henry Pluckrose

Photography: Chris Fairclough

FRANKLIN WATTS
New York/London/Toronto/Sydney

Copyright © 1991
Franklin Watts

Franklin Watts Inc
387 Park Avenue South
New York, NY 10016

Library of Congress Cataloging-in-Publication Data

Lancaster, John, 1930—
    Art with found materials / by John Lancaster.
        p.   cm.—(Fresh start)
    Includes index.
    Summary: Provides instructions for constructing simple sculptures
out of different types of natural objects, such as pinecones and
twigs.
    ISBN 0-531-14204-3
    1. Found objects (Art)—Juvenile literature.   [1. Found objects
(Art)   2. Handicraft.]   I. Title.   II. Series: Fresh start (London,
England)
N7433.7.L36   1992
745.5—dc20   91-2875
                                                                 CIP AC

Design: K and Co

Editor: Jenny Wood

Typeset by Lineage Ltd,
Watford, England

Printed in Belgium

Contents

This book describes activities which use the following:

Brushes (watercolor or hog hair)

Cardboard (a variety of sizes cut from cardboard boxes which you can obtain from your local supermarket)

Cardboard boxes (several, to cut up; two or three to use as storage containers for your equipment and models; one to use as a spray box)

Chocolate boxes (or other small boxes to use as bases for models)

Cutting board (any flat piece of wood, particleboard or formica, larger than 4in x 6in)

Cutting knife (a matte knife or craft knife with a sharp blade)

Drill

Glue (strong adhesive such as Elmer's Glue)

Masking tape

Modeling clay

Natural forms (a selection – acorns, bark, cattails, chestnuts, dried grasses, leaves, loofahs, nuts, pinecones, sand, seed heads from dried flowers, shells, sponges, stones and pebbles, twigs)

Paints – acrylic
– colored spray paint in a range of colors
– gold, bronze and/or silver spray paint
– household paint or lacquer

Pitcher (small, or watering can)

Ruler (12in metal ruler)

Sandpaper

Saw (junior hacksaw, fretsaw or coping saw with which to cut wooden bases to size)

Scissors

Tin lids (from discarded jelly jars etc.; plastic lids and plastic beakers can also be used as bases)

Tray (pottery or tin)

Water

Wood – short lengths of timber, for example, 2in x 2in
– small pieces of particleboard or plywood

1 Some of the equipment you will need when making the sculptures in this book.

In this book you will be shown how to design and construct simple three-dimensional models. Such models are called sculptures.

If this is the first time you are attempting this kind of artwork, read through each section carefully. By following the instructions and ideas, you will soon find that you are able to produce small, worthwhile sculptures.

You should be able to find the natural materials listed without difficulty, and at no cost. Your biggest expense will be on spray paint and glue, but use oddments of household paints to color your sculptures if necessary.

Some hints

Always wear a smock, apron or old shirt to protect your clothes when you are working. Work at a bench, a table covered with newspaper or plastic, or on an area of floor protected by a sheet of particleboard, plastic, or brown craft paper.

From time to time a sculptor will look at the piece he or she is making, viewing it from the front and the back as well as from each side. These are vital stages, because they allow the sculptor to watch the progress of his or her sculpture from every possible angle. Do the same thing yourself. It will help you keep the proportions of each sculpture right and therefore allow the sculpture to grow well as a "designed" object.

Thinking in this way demands what are called "building and constructing" skills. The more you work, and the more critical you are of what you do, the more these skills will develop.

Do a drawing of each sculpture before you start, showing what you intend the finished sculpture to look like. Do a second drawing once the sculpture is complete. Compare the two drawings.

When cutting wood, cardboard, twigs or other materials with a saw or sharp knife, take great care. Always work on your cutting board. Never point the knife at anyone. Never cut towards your body. Put the knife in a safe place after use, and replace the blade cover.

The first thing to do is go for a nature walk with an adult or friend and look for a range of natural forms. You should be able to find these in your backyard or local park, in fields or at the beach. Take care not to damage any trees, shrubs, plants or fences. Take a suitable container (for example, a plastic bag) with you in which to carry back your finds.

Some natural forms for you to find

Some of the items on this list will be used for the activities suggested in this book. Collect these, but look around for others not on the list as well.

Acorns	Pinecones
Cattails	Sand
Chestnuts	Shells
Leaves	Small stones
Nuts	Sponges
Pieces of bark	Twigs

1 A selection of natural forms.

Each sculpture you make will require a firm base on which to stand. Although various sizes of bases are suggested throughout the book, you can vary these depending upon the kinds of materials you use.

Prepare some bases in advance of making your sculptures. Here are some ideas.

1 Saw two or three wooden bases from a length of timber and smooth them with sandpaper.

2 Cut some pieces of particleboard or plywood, and sand these to give a smooth, even surface.

3 Cut a number of squares from thick cardboard.

4 Collect a few small cardboard boxes.

5 Look around for other objects such as tin lids and small plastic beakers which could be used as bases.

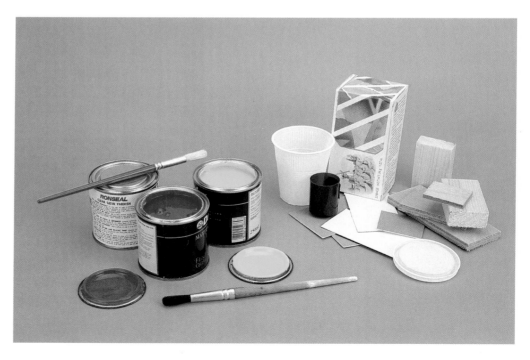

6 Color some of your bases.

Many natural forms come into being through natural growth or the effects of weathering. They are like beautiful sculptures, and are often rich in color, pattern and texture. These features combine with the shape of a form to create something which is pleasing to look at.

You will need a collection of different natural forms, a selection of wooden bases and/or containers on and in which to display your natural forms, and glue.

1 Select a natural form and display it on a polished wooden base. This rock fell from crumbling cliffs into the sea below. It was turned into a piece of natural sculpture by the eroding effects of sea-water and sand grinding out holes in its surface.

2 Pick up and handle the natural form you are working with before you decide on the base or container on or in which you are going to display it. Look at its color and pattern, and feel its texture.

3 Sometimes a base is not required, and you can place your selected natural form on a bare surface. Do you know what this object is? It is tumbleweed from a prairie out west, and is hard and spiky to touch.

4 Try grouping similar natural forms together.

5 Try grouping different natural forms together. Those which have similar or complementary shapes, colors and patterns often seem to blend well. You may have to glue the natural forms in position.

12

6 A finished "sculptural piece."

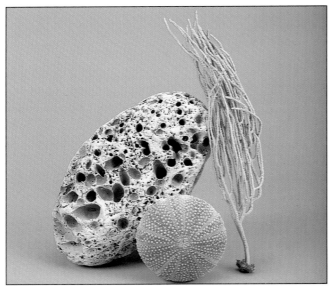

7 A simple arrangement of different natural forms.

A twig sculpture

Small, grotesquely-formed or gnarled twigs are interesting natural sculptures. They can be displayed on a base, or as a mobile sculpture suspended from a ceiling or beam by thin nylon thread. Display them singly or in groups of two or three.

You will need a gnarled twig, paints and paintbrushes.

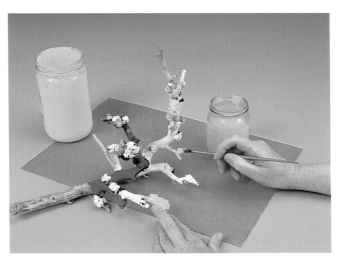

1 Some twigs look best painted in only one color. Others benefit from being painted in two or more colors as this gives greater emphasis to their twisted shapes.

2 A finished twig sculpture.

A linear sculpture

Linear sculptures use simple lines to create an effect. You will need a strong wooden base, some dried stalks or twigs, glue, pinecones, paints and paintbrushes. Make the base for this standing sculpture by sawing a square piece from the end of a length of timber and smoothing it with fine sandpaper.

1 Cut or break off six lengths of stalks or twigs. These can range from approximately 10in-14in.

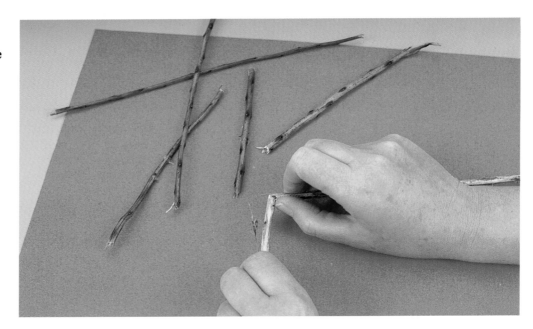

2 Cut or break off some shorter lengths, ranging from approximately 4in-8in. Glue a number of these shorter pieces across two of the longer pieces, to make a ladder-like construction. Make two more "ladders" from the remaining pieces of stalk or twig. Allow the glue to harden.

3 Glue the three "ladders" onto the wooden base, each one on a different side. Allow the glue to harden.

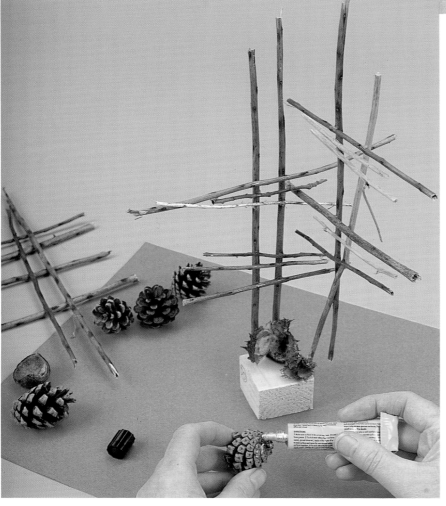

4 Decorate the top of the wooden base with pinecones or other appropriate natural forms.

5 The finished linear sculpture. Color the sculpture by painting the stalks or twigs in three different colors, or by spraying the whole model with gold, silver or bronze paint.

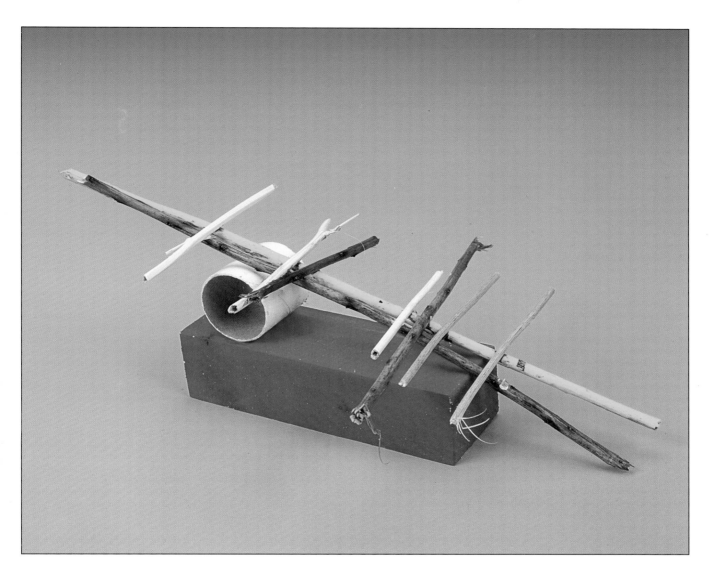

6 Make a different type of linear sculpture by gluing a short length of painted cardboard tube on top of a painted base. Lay a ladder of twigs over the tube and glue it firmly in position. This sculpture can be free-standing or mounted on a wall.

Late summer and autumn are good times to collect seed heads, nuts, acorns and pinecones. You will often find them lying on the ground around the bases of many different kinds of shrubs and trees. If you use such natural forms imaginatively you will produce some interesting sculptural models.

You will need a selection of seed heads and chestnut shells, wooden bases, glue, paints and paintbrushes.

1 Glue a half-opened chestnut shell onto a small wooden base. Hold it in place until the glue hardens. Add more chestnut shells, arranging them in such a way that you produce a standing model.

2 The chestnut shells in this sculpture were twisted to one side as they were stuck together. This has produced an interesting shape. When the sculpture was finished it was painted yellow. Do you think this makes the sculpture more interesting, or are the shells more attractive left in their natural state?

3 A close-up of part of a chestnut shell sculpture.

4 Two small models made from seed heads.

An acorn sculpture

To make this sculpture you will need a wooden block (about 6in long) to use as a base, some large acorns, glue, a pinecone, and seeds or pieces of dried grass.

1 Glue the first acorn onto the top of the base.

2 Add more acorns, arranging these to form a pattern.

3 When the acorns are secure, stand the wooden block upright. Complete the sculpture by adding a pinecone to the top.

4 The finished sculpture.

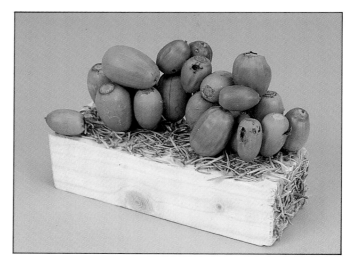

5 Give the surface of your wooden base a more interesting texture by gluing seeds or pieces of dried grass onto it.

6 The base of this acorn sculpture has two textured sides.

7 Here, chestnuts are being used to make a relief sculpture.

You will need two wooden bases, pinecones, glue, spray paint, a large cardboard box, a drill, and a twig between 5in and 8in in length.

1 For the first sculpture, glue a row of cones onto a wooden base. Decide for yourself on the length of the base.

2 Position the last pinecone at a different angle from the others, to give variety to your sculpture.

3 When the glue has set, color your sculpture with spray paint. Make a spray box from a large cardboard box and place your sculpture inside, to protect you and your work area.

4 The finished
sculpture.

5 The second sculpture is more difficult to make. Begin by preparing a painted wooden base. Drill a hole in the top face of the base.

6 Glue five or six pinecones to the twig.

26

7 Position the
pinecones on different
sides of the twig, for
variety.

8 Allow the glue to set,
then slot the twig into
the hole on the base.
Secure the twig in this
position with a dab of
glue.

9 Glue two or three pinecones together to form a small group.

10 Arrange a number of these pinecone groups around the upright twig on the base. Glue them securely into position.

11 The finished sculpture. Two of the pinecones have been colored red, for effect.

Sponges and loofahs are found in the sea in some parts of the world. If you go to such places on vacation, then you may discover one or two on the beach. On the other hand, you may have an old sponge or loofah at home that you can use.

These natural forms are full of three-dimensional holes and textures. They are interesting to look at and to touch. If you squeeze a dry sponge it will feel firm. Do the same when it is wet, and it will feel soft and "spongy." A loofah feels different. It is scratchy, and harder than a sponge.

You will need an old sponge or loofah, a saw or craft knife, glue and a base.

1 Use the saw or craft knife to cut your sponge or loofah into small pieces. Make sure the pieces are dry before you start work on your sculpture.

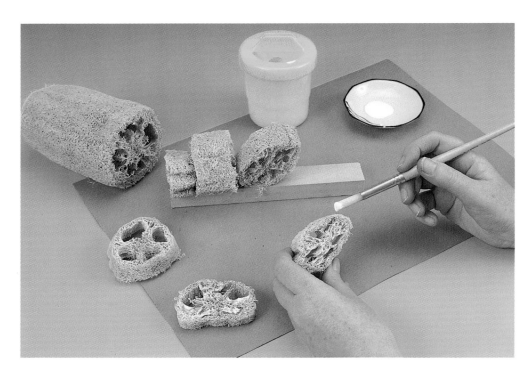

2 Glue the pieces onto the base you have chosen.

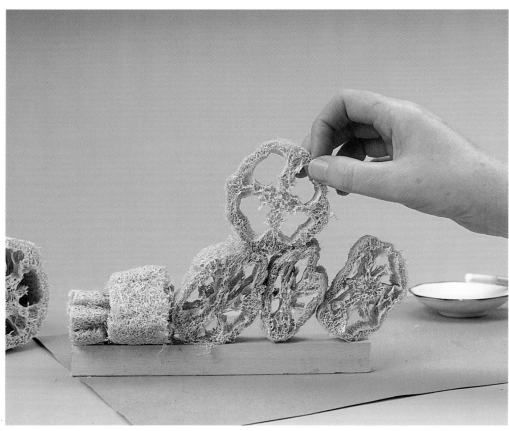

3 Arrange the pieces in an interesting pattern.

Try spray-painting the small pieces of sponge or loofah before you arrange them on the base. Paint two pieces in gold, two in red, and the rest in a color of your choice.

Use different types of bases for your sponge or loofah sculptures. Try a tin lid, a plastic lid or an upturned plastic pot instead of wood.

4 In the unpainted sculpture shown here, cuts were made into a fairly large piece of loofah. The loofah was then opened out and glued onto a painted wooden base. Another small piece of loofah, cut in a different way, was then positioned in the center. Its form contrasts nicely with the main loofah piece.

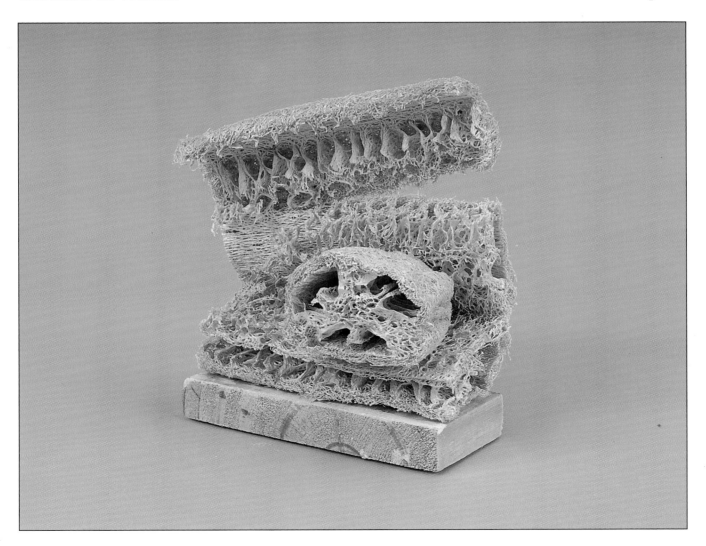

Now that you have made a number of sculptures, here are some other ideas for you to try:

A sand tray water erosion sculpture

You will need a large tray, a short length of wood, stones and pebbles, sand, a piece of bark or one or two twigs, a pitcher or small watering can, and water. The tray shown in the photographs is a pottery one. A tin tray will do just as well, or you can make your own from a piece of particleboard or plywood approximately 24in x 12in with a wooden lip (1in deep) all around.

1 Place the tray on the ground, on a solid concrete floor or on an area of floor covered with a plastic sheet. Raise one end of the tray between ¾in and 1½in away from the surface by placing a short length of wood underneath. Use pebbles or small stones instead of wood, if necessary.

2 Scoop some sand into the tray.

3 Form the sand into small hills, valleys and flat areas. Try to make your sand tray look like a landscape.

4 Lay some pebbles and stones on the sand, then add the piece of bark or the twigs to create the effect of fallen tree trunks.

Rain showers erode our own landscapes over many weeks, months and even years. Look around to see the effects of rain and wind upon the fields, hills or coastal areas near where you live.

How does your own "eroded landscape" compare with erosion in the outside world?

5 When you have created your landscape, gently dribble some water onto it. Using the pitcher or small watering can will help you control the flow of water. Make sure the water does not run out of the lower end of the tray, and quickly mop up any water which does escape.

6 Repeat this process from time to time over a period of three or four days. Observe what happens to the sand in the tray and how the water affects your small landscape. Keep a notebook with sketches, maps, photographs and written notes about what happens.

Shells

When you go to the beach, make a collection of shells, large and small. Sort them out carefully when you return home.

1 Make a "relief" sculpture by arranging shells in straight lines or in circles on a strong base of plywood or thick cardboard 8in x 8in.

2 Using a strong adhesive, cover the four sides of a strong cube (either wood or cardboard) with small shells. When the shells are attached securely, add more to the top of the cube.

3 Glue small shells all over an inverted plastic beaker or yogurt cup. Spray your finished sculpture with gold, silver or colored paint.

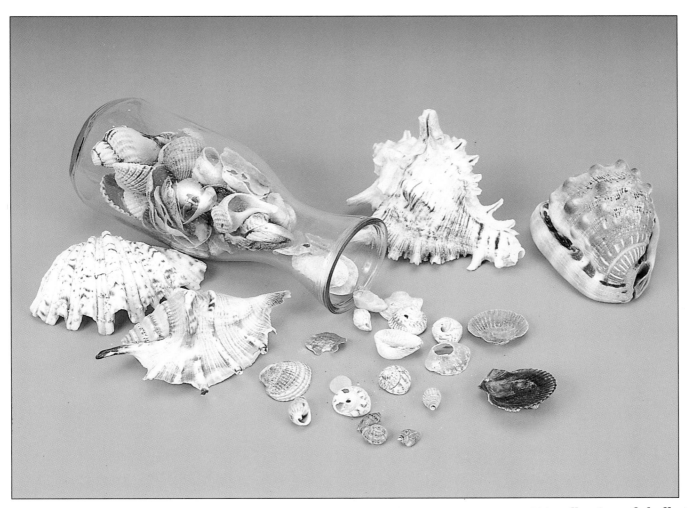

7 A collection of shells.

Clay models

The models in pictures **8, 9** and **10** were made with clay. One was based on seed heads, another on a pebble. Which one was based on a mushroom?

Using modeling clay, make one or two models yourself. Use a small stone, shell or piece of loofah to help inspire what you do.

8 A clay model.

9 A clay model.

10 A clay model.

Bark

Different species of tree have bark that varies in pattern and texture. Some are smooth, while others have rough surfaces. Look for some pieces of bark which have fallen away from old tree trunks or branches. These may be rough and deeply etched.

ON NO ACCOUNT SHOULD YOU DAMAGE TREES TO OBTAIN BARK.

Think of ways of using bark to make interesting sculptures. You can keep the pieces of bark whole, or break them into smaller portions.

11 A tree bark sculpture.

Now have fun thinking up ideas of your own.

Most of the materials mentioned in this book are easy to obtain. Many of them – particularly the various kinds of natural materials – can be collected in the local environment near to where you live. If you are lucky enough to have a backyard, you can search in it for wood, twigs and other natural materials. If you live in the country, you will have trees, bushes, fields and woods in which to look. Those who live in cities can often go into a park for their finds.

Materials such as wood can be bought in local stores or in home centers. Paints, paintbrushes, spray paints, crayons and inks may be obtained in stationery or art materials stores.

Larger quantities of materials, as well as certain items of equipment, can be ordered through suppliers of artists' materials. The following suppliers accept mail order:
SAX ARTS & CRAFTS
P.O. Box 2002
Milwaukee, WI 53201
414-272-4900
1-800-242-4911

DICK BLICK ART MATERIALS
P.O. Box 1267
Galesburg, IL 61401
309-343-6181
1-800-447-8192

It may be difficult to find books concerned with making art from found materials. Visit your local library and ask whether they have any books concerned with nature crafts and sculpture, so that you can see what artists such as Henry Moore and Barbara Hepworth created. Also ask to see books concerned with natural scenery and natural forms – rocks, bones, shells, cliffs, sand patterns, etc. Take a little time to look for photographs of these things in magazines and newspapers. If you cut them out you will soon have a useful collection of resource material to refer to. Such a collection will be invaluable as you begin to try to develop your own ideas.

PRINTED IN BELGIUM BY proost INTERNATIONAL BOOK PRODUCTION